This book belongs to:

Lucky Bride is:

Important Dates

Cinifan Date

Nikkah Date

Mendhi Date

Wedding Date

Important Dates

Important Dates

Important Dates

Bridesmaids List

Bridesmaids List

Things I need to do

Things I need to do

Things I need to do

Things I need to do

Things I need to do

Things I need to do

Things I need to do

Things I need to do

Things I need to do

Things I need to do

Book Makeup artist

mua and hair stylist:
DATE:
TIME:
PAYMENT:
DEPOSIT:
Number of people:

mua and hair stylist:
DATE:
TIME:
PAYMENT:
DEPOSIT:
Number of people:

Book Makeup artist

mua and hair stylist:
DATE:
TIME:
PAYMENT:
DEPOSIT:
number of people:

mua and hair stylist:
DATE:
TIME:
PAYMENT:
DEPOSIT:
number of people:

Bridesmaids outfit for Nikkah
Ideas

Budget:

Bridesmaids outfit for Mendhi Ideas

Budget:

Bridesmaids outfit for Turmeric party

Budget:

Bridesmaids outfit for Wedding Ideas

Budget:

Bridesmaids outfit for:

Budget:

Bridesmaids outfit for:

Budget:

Mendhi Dance rhersals

List of songs:

Mendhi Dance rehearsals

Mendhi Dance rhersals

Mendhi Dance rhersals

Mendhi Thaals

Mendhi Thaals

Take a Break!

Keep hydrated + keep up with your skincare for a beautiful glow and flawless base for that makeup! Don't forget to treat yourself and eat properly. Maybe plan a cosy movie night....if you're up for more planning x

Wedding gate signs

"£10,000 or the bride goes home"

"No money? DhulaBYE"

"No money no Rani"

"Pay up Mister or you ain't taking our sister"

Wedding gate signs ideas and materialis

Wedding gate signs

Nikkah Contract

Groom agrees to the following:

1.

2.

3.

4.

5.

6.

7.

8.

9.

10.

Nikkah Contract

Groom agrees to the following:

Bride...Look away
Bridesmaids...Goodluck!

Bridal shower

Date:

Place:

Theme:

Outfit for bride:

Food:

Games:

Number of people:

Who's invited?

1.

2.

3.

4.

5.

6.

7.

8.

9.

10.

Who's invited?

Gifts for bride?

- Spa treatments
- skincare products
- perfume
- Hair Straighter
- Hair blow dryer
- Islamic Books
- Personalised Prayer mat etc...
- Pajamas
- Getaway gift
- Makeup
- Create short memory film
-
-
-
-
-
-
-
-

Dress Code

Bridal shower Notes

Bridal shower Notes

Shopping List

Shopping List

Shopping List

Shopping List

Shopping List

Nashta Day
(Breakfast after the wedding)

Nashta Day

Nayor (bride comes back home)

1. Welcoming drinks and desi sweets

2. Snacks

3. Games & movies

4. Food

5. Decorate Bedroom: candles, fairy light, chocolates & drinks etc...

6. Dont forget to prank the groom e.g salt in tea x

Notes for Nayor

Notes x

Notes x

Notes x

Notes x

Notes x

Notes x

Notes x

Reflection

How was the whole wedding process?

Which function was your favorite?

Your favorite outfit was?

Reflection

Did the bride become bridezilla?

Did you cry at any point? Lol

Who's next in line to get married?...
Goodluck if it's you!

Reflection

Did everything go smoothly? (Does an Asian wedding ever lol)

whats one thing that went terrible?

who annoyed you 100% during this (Its just me and you)

Reflection

Has an aunty approached you or The other bridesmaids for a proposal? lol

Tell me who messed up the dance at the mendhi? and then snap them your answer because they owe you milkshakes.

Did your outfits go to plan?

Reflection

who was the laziest bridesmaid?

who was the most creative bridesmaid?

who was the perfectionist?

who was the extremely emotional bridesmaid?

Reflection

what advice would you give to the bride
on starting her new chapter?

what tip would you give to the Groom?

Reflection

Drop down a cute message for the bride then send it her...

Reflection

write down your feelings women!

The end...until

Gets married! x

This may or may not be a hint.

Printed in Great Britain
by Amazon